Legends of Ten Chinese Traditional Festivals

Illustrator   Zh

Dolphin Books Beijing

Editor : Li Shufen

Designer : Fang Yongming

Third Edition 2003

ISBN 7-80051-522-2/J.708

Published by Dolphin Books

24 Baiwanzhuang Road, Beijing 100037, China

Tel: 86-10-68326332

Spring Festival

The Spring Festival is the lunar Chinese New Year. Every family sets off firecrackers and puts up couplets on their gates to usher in a happy life in the coming year.

Long, long ago, there was a ferocious demon called *nian*. It did evil things everywhere.

The Heavenly God locked this demon into remote mountains and only allowed him to go out once a year.

Shortly after twelve months had passed, *nian* came out of the mountains.

Gathering together, people discussed how to deal with him. Some said that *nian* was afraid of the red color, flames, and noises.

So people put up red couplets on their gates, set off firecrackers, and kept on beating gongs and drums.

The demon *nian* trembled with fear.

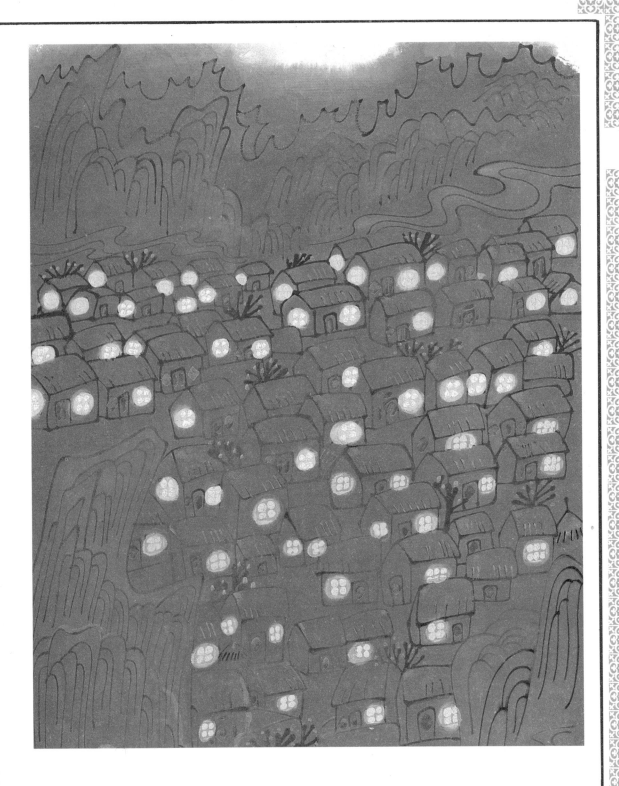

Night fell and every house was brightly lit.

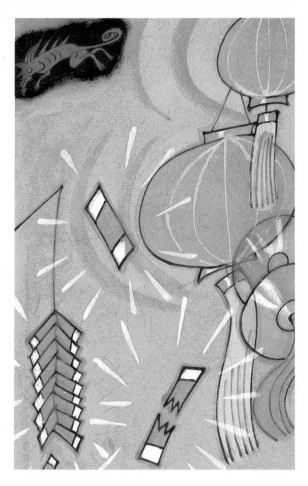

Nian was terrified. He fled into the mountains and didn't dare to come out.

Nian was thus subdued, and the custom of celebrating the lunar New Year was passed down from then.

Lantern Festival

The fifteenth day of the first lunar month is the day of the Lantern Festival. This festival dates back over 2,000 years.

The Jade Emperor in Heaven lived comfortably, but he felt very lonely.

When he learned that people on earth lived happily, he got quite angry.

He decided to send the Magic Goose who could breathe out flames to burn up the world on the fifteenth day of the first lunar month.

A kind-hearted maid of the Heavenly Palace went down to the world hurriedly and told everybody about the news.

A clever man got an idea. He called up his fellow citizens to make red lanterns immediately.

The maid also told people that once the Magic Goose was caged, it would no longer be able to breathe out flames.

Shortly after it landed on the earth, and before it got the chance to start a fire, the Magic Goose was caught and caged.

People then lit their lanterns and set off fireworks and fire-crackers. When the Jade Emperor saw the flame, he thought it was the fire set by the Magic Goose, so he became very happy.

In fact, people were holding lanterns to celebrate their victory. Later, when this day came, every family made lanterns and held them. So the fifteenth day of the first lunar month be-came known as the Lantern Festival.

Dragon Head Festival

The Dragon Head Festival, celebrated in rural China, falls on the second day of the second lunar month. The Chinese proverb "on the second day of the second lunar month the dragon raises its head" has a story behind it.

Long ago, in an ancient time, there was a drought along the Yellow River that lasted for three years. All the rivers had dried up and people suffered a lot.

There was a mountain called Dragon Ax on the bank of the Yellow River. At the foot of the mountain lived a young couple. The man was called Qiang Wa and the woman Long Hua.

Both Qiang Wa and Long Hua were determined to look for sources of water to help their fellow villagers. An old man told them that they could find water at the bottom of the Golden Dragon Pond.

Qiang Wa and Long Hua were not afraid of difficulties or hardships.They kept on crawling until they reached the bottom of the Golden Dragon Pond.

They didn't stop digging for forty-nine days. One day they dug out a white, round stone from the earth. With one roll, the stone suddenly turned into a white dove and flew up.

The dove landed on the side of the pond and turned into an old man with a white beard. The old man said, "Good children, hurry to the top of the Dragon Ax Mountain and try to get the mountain-cutting ax. With this ax you can cut through the mountain and let in the water." Having said this, the old man turned into a cloud of white smoke and disappeared.

After many, many hardships, Qiang Wa and Long Hua reached the top of the Dragon Ax Mountain. There they saw a small temple.

They went into the temple and found a big ax. Shouldering it, they hurried back to the Golden Dragon Pond.

Qiang Wa swung one blow at th[e]
mountain, and with a loud noise,[a]
stream of spring water spurted ou[t.]
A golden dragon rushed to the sk[y]
and at once raindrops fell to th[e]
ground.

So people named the second day of the
second lunar month the Dragon Head
Festival in honor of the golden dragon.

Clear and Bright Festival

The Clear and Bright Festival is celebrated every year on a day in early April. On that day, people usually go on outings, pay respects to the ancestors at their tombs, wear flowers, and plant willow twigs into the ground.

During the Spring and Autumn Period some 2,500 years ago, Chong Er, son of the Duke of the State of Jin, was forced to live in exile for some nineteen years. But later he became the Duke.

He granted titles and fiefdoms to tho who had followed him throughout h exile.

One follower called Jie Zhitui was forgotten by Chong Er. Jie Zhitui then Carried his mother on his back and hid in the Miansham Mountain.

Someone reminded Chong Er of Jie Zhitui.

Chong Er sent people to look for Jie, but they all failed because the Mianshan Mountain was too large.

Then one man suggested, "Set the mountain on fire, and Jie Zhitui will certainly come out." Chong Er ordered a fire to be set to the mountain.

The fire spread all over the mountain, but Jie Zhitui still would not come out. Finally he and his mother were burned to death.

Chong Er felt very sad. He issued an order that every family put out their kitchen fire and eat cold food that very day.

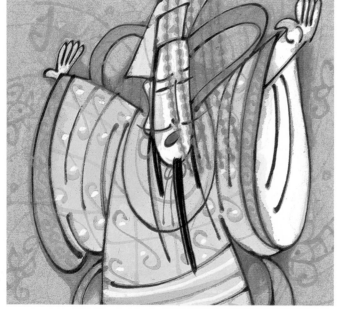

The custom of putting out the kitchen fire on the Clear and Bright Festival has vanished, but the habits of planting willow twigs and paying respects to ancestors at their tombs have continued to the present day.

Dragon Boat Festival

The Dragon Boat Festival falls on the fifth day of the fifth lunar month. On that day, every family in rural China eats *zongzi* (glutinous rice wrapped in reed leaves). It is also the custom to hang wormwood and carry "fragrant pouches" made of bits of cloth wound with colored silk threads.

Why do people eat *zongzi*? ... said to be done in memory of ... Yuan.

Qu Yuan was a high-ranking official of the State of Chu during the Warring States Period (475-221 B.C.).He had made great contributions to the state.

The corrupt officials of the court slandered Qu Yuan until finally he was removed from office by the Duke.

Later he was banished and led a wandering life.

He still loved his country and people and was overwhelmed with sadness.

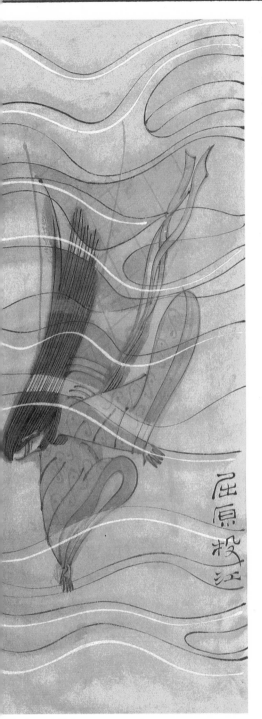

屈原投江

Qu Yuan drowned himself in the Miluo River on the fifth day of the fifth lunar month upon the news of his country being conquered.

汨羅江

e people of the State of Chu threw
e into the river as a sacrifice to him.

Later they were afraid that the fish and shrimps would eat the rice. So they wrapped the food in reed leaves and wound silk threads around the packets before dropping them into the river.

People also used bits of cloth to make "fragrant pouches" wound round with colored silk threads and carried them. They hung calamus and wormwood, which are two medicinal herbs, on their gates to symbolize a knife and sword to conquer evil.

Double Seventh Night

The Double Seventh Night falls on the seventh night of the seventh lunar month. On that night girls hold needle-threading competitions to see who has nimble fingers. The competitions are held in honor of the weaving maid of the Heavenly Palace.

he weaving maid in the Heavenly Pal- e wove celestial brocade for the Queen other of the Western Heaven every day.

n earth there lived a cowherd who led a iserable life. He had only one compan- n — an old ox.

The weaving maid fell in love with the cowherd because he was so hardworking. Stealthily, she went down to the world and married him. Later she gave birth to a boy and a girl, and the family lived happily together.

The Queen Mother of the Western Heaven got very angry and ordered troops from the heaven to bring back the weaving maid.

The heavenly force captured the weaving maid. Holding the children, the cowherd chased after them on the back of the old ox.

The Queen Mother of the Western Heaven plucked a gold pin from her hair and drew a line with it in the air. Immediately a celestial river appeared in the sky. The cowherd and the weaving maid were separated by the river.

On the seventh night of the seventh lunar month every year, magpies fly to the river and form a bridge over it, and the cowherd and weaving maid meet in the middle of the bridge.

On that night, girls beg the weaving maid to pass them skill at weaving. They also rejoice at the couple's reunion.

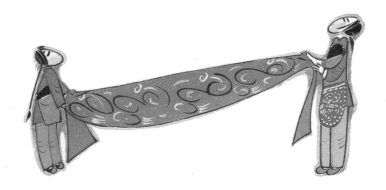

The Mid-Autumn Festival falls on the fifteenth day of the eighth lunar month. On that day every family eats mooncakes. Children usually buy different kinds of clay toys.

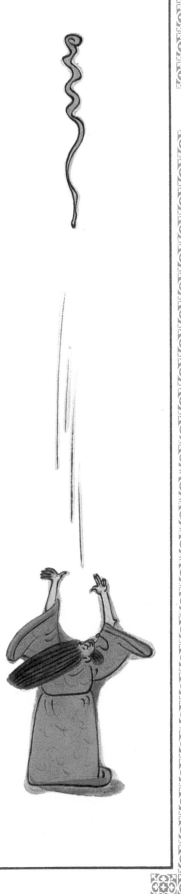

The story below is one of the many legends about the
Mid-Autumn Festival.

A Taoist priest said to the Tang Emperor Xuan Zong,"I
can take you to the moon palace." Having said this, he
threw his walking stick into the sky.

The stick turned into a long bridge. The Tang
Emperor followed the priest onto the passage
and entered the moon palace.

In the moon palace, the Tang Emperor saw a Jade Rabbit pounding medicinal herbs in a mortar and a group of fairy maidens dancing and playing music. Fascinated by the music the Tang Emperor tried to remember the tunes by heart.

After returning to the world, the emperor composed a song-and-dance piece called "Rainbow Petticoats and Feather Dresses" after the tunes he brought back in his memory from the moon palace.

Double Ninth Day

The ninth day of the ninth lunar month is known as the Double Ninth Day. On that day people usually go traveling or climbing mountains.

During the Eastern Han Dynasty (25-220 A.D.) there was a Taoist priest called Fei Changfang. He knew magic arts and could drive out evil spirits.

One day Fei Changfang warned his disciple Huan Jing that the spirit of disaster would visit the world on the ninth day of the ninth lunar month. Fei told Huan Jing to go to the countryside and conquer it.

Fei gave Huan Jing a parcel containing the leaves of a medicinal cornel plant and a jug of chrysanthemum wine. He asked his disciple to take them to the people.

Riding on a white crane, Huan Jing descended to the world.

He led people up a mountain and gave everyone a cornel leaf and a drink of chrysanthemum wine. These would prevent the disaster from getting near.

Disaster came to the village. It found no one there. Catching sight of the people on the mountain it rushed to the mountain.

Unexpectedly it caught a whiff of chrysanthemum wine and cornel plant. Hesiating to go ahead, it was stabbed by Huan Jing and fell to the ground.

Since then people have gone traveling or climbing, bringing along chrysanthemum wine and twigs of the cornel plant, on the ninth day of the ninthg lunar ninth.

Laba Festival

On the eighth day of the twelfth lunar month, the Laba Festival is celebrated. On that day every family eats *laba* congee (The twelfth lunar month is called the *la* month, which means a world of ice and snow).

Long, long ago, there was a family of four: an old couple and a young couple who lived happily together.

The old couple did all the housework. They didn't let the young couple do anything, for fear of them getting tired.

The young couple led an easy life with everything provided
for them. They did not know how to do anything.

Later the old couple died. After eating up
all the food that had been stored in the
house, the young couple sold their house
and was left with only half a broken straw
shed.

...r came. The couple suffered from cold
...unger in their poor shelter.

On the eighth day of the twelfth
lunar month, when they could
bear the hunger no more, they
scrounged up a little grain from
the corners of the shed and
cooked a pot of congee.

A gust of wind blew down their shed and they were crushed to death.

People learned about this later.In order to teach their children about the sad fate of that lazy couple, they would cook congee with all kinds of grains and, while eating it, tell the story.

Kitchen God Day

On the twenty-third day of the twelfth lunar month, children eat melon-shaped candies and adults offer melon-shaped candies as a sacrifice to the Kitchen God.

Long, long ago, there was a lord. He was very fond of eating. He had soon tasted all the delicious foods in his palace.

Later he went out of his palace to look for good things to eat.

He came to a woman's house and begged for food.

He soon ate up the sugar cakes
the woman had baked.

Then he asked the woman to go to his palace with him and bake sugar cakes for him every day.

The woman wouldn't hear of it. The lord then threatened to drag her to the palace.

The woman lost her temper and slapped him on the face with all her might. The slap sent the lord flying to the wall behind the kitchen sink.

The woman said to the lord, "Stop being such a glutton! Stay there and watch other people eat!" From then on the lord couldn't get down. Later he became the Kitchen God.

People worried that the Kitchen God might report bad things about them to the Heavenly God. So every year, before the Spring festival, they would post a new picture of the Kitchen God and offer him melon-shaped candies. Now people no longer post the pictures, but children still get melon-shaped candies to eat.